How to Write a Bestseller

Published by Arthur Zulu

© Copyright, Arthur Zulu

Fifth Edition, 2015

ISBN-13: 978-1484911198

DEDICATION

To My Mother, Georgina

"He whose face gives no light, shall never become a star."—William Blake

CONTENTS

CHAPTER 1

WHAT TO KNOW ABOUT WRITING

"Dare to know."—Emmanuel Kant

Do you want to write a bestseller and become rich and famous? Yes, you can, if you really believe in yourself, and sit down to translate your dream into reality. The sad thing though is that some are defeated even before they pen down that first dreaded sentence. But know that fear, doubt and indecision are the greatest enemies of success; and if these have been your lot in life, then you need a wake-up call. Cast away all negative thoughts, and tell yourself this moment that you want to reach the star—you want to write a bestseller—and I tell you that you can. If, however, you have not yet believed in the inestimable power in you to be a star writer, then I am sorry you are WASTING your time reading this book, and should STOP right here!

But if you believe like I do that everything you write will be a blockbuster, then read the questions which I had once asked, and which will help you on your way to stardom.

What am I to write about?

That's a naive question. There are many subjects to write on. All the books that have ever been written have not tapped into man's inexhaustible fountain of knowledge. Look at science for example, and ask: Suppose scientists stopped trying, would you be reading this as an electronic book on some device, a phone or laptop? Or would man have been thinking of colonizing planet Mars or of putting up a floating vacation resort for holiday makers in space with a window view of the earth?

But despite all these scientists have not discovered all the species of living things and the numerous stars and galaxies in the expanding universe. Yet, they have not stopped trying, and maybe someday we may have to travel back in time to the moment of the Big Bang! So, why do you say, *What am I to write about?*

Authors have had inspiration to write great books while sitting in a bus, walking the woods, contemplating nature on the beach, watching a movie or by reading a book.

So you see that writing is thinking. Think and you will *discover* things. But suppose you don't know what to write, you may say like many diffident people:

I did not study the art of writing

Know that you do not need to attend a writing school in order to write a bestseller. The greatest writers didn't attend writing schools. All you need is the power of imagination.

You may agree with that and say instead:

I am not highly educated

If by education you mean having some kind of high school training then I will say that you don't need to be educated in the conventional use of the word to write a blockbuster. Tell me, did all the great writers go to school? William Shakespeare was not an educated man and Charles Dickens taught himself writing. Yet, both were literary czars.

But then comes the question:

Will I make money?

Of course, you must know that not all writers live off their writing. But we are talking of writing mega yield titles. And if you write a bestseller, it means that your book will be everywhere and be read by most persons. It therefore follows as a writer of a best-selling book that you will make money, get contracts from publishers to write, give talks and pocket away money, and go on to win prizes!

Now, you are going to be known.

But I don't want to be famous

You can't help it as a world-class writer. You will be known everywhere. Does that frighten you?

But who will publish me?

Write first, and think of getting published, later. The truth though is that most traditional publishers will reject you.

But after you have been published, after your work has become a bestseller and everyone is talking about you, the same publishers who rejected you will come begging for your work and offering you advance fees to write for them to publish!

However, the good news today is that you may not have to go that route because there are several online publishing outlets, and some are free!

How can I write a bestseller?

That's the best question of all. But before you write that bestseller, let's see writers who have written masterpieces and why they wrote them.

CHAPTER 2

WHY THEY WROTE BESTSELLERS

"Of all the arts in which the wise excel, Nature's chief masterpiece is writing well." —John Sheffield

Many writers wrote well and their books became commercial successes. I have presented a selection of writers of both sexes from diverse lands and of various time periods who wrote in different genres, and giving reasons for their acclaim.

Archer, Jeffrey

Jeffrey Howard Archer was born on April 15, 1940 in Western Super Mare, England. He became a politician after his education at Oxford, and decided to write himself out of debt when his business collapsed. This gave birth to the instant successful novel, *Not a Penny More, Not a Penny Less.* Other masterpieces followed among which are *First Among Equals, Shall We Tell the President?, Kane and Abel,* and *A Matter of Honor.* He became so rich and held his readers spell- bound for over two decades. Why?

He wrote on familiar topics—politics, crime, and sex. His characters also seem real—ambitious and fighting people.

He also used known people in international politics as characters, which gave his story more visibility. They included Margaret Thatcher, Ted Kennedy, Saddam Hussein, and Rupert Murdock.

Archer is also very descriptive and likes to put his readers in suspense.

The beloved writer who is married with children got a four-year jail term for perjury. Ever since, it seems that he is no longer first among equals.

Bronte, Emily

Born on July 30, 1818 at Thornton, Bradford, in bleak Yorkshire moors, England, Emily Bronte was the fifth child of six children. She and her family members had a poor, harsh beginning, and reared under the tyranny of their pastor-father. In order to escape their unhappy lives, the children took to writing, with Emily and Anne writing poetry and stories for their imaginary world of Gondal.

Of all the three sisters who wrote books—Emily, Charlotte, and Anne—Emily stands out as the best, though her work did not gain equal recognition as Charlotte's autobiographical *Jane Eyre* in her life time. The works of the Bronte sisters cannot be compared to any other work in English literature because they arose out of personal emotion.

But by far, the greatest of them all is Emily's *Wuthering Heights*, her only novel. This novel, the violent tale of love and revenge, has been dubbed the most imaginative novel in English literature. What was it that made it so?

Emily Bronte had rich imagination and this is a great asset for any aspiring writer. Furthermore, she wrote on romance, and stories of love and revenge make bestsellers any day.

She died on December 19, 1848 at 30.

Brown, Dan

Dan Brown was born June 22, 1964 in Exeter, New Hampshire, US, the oldest of three children. He attended Amherst College where he was a member of Psi Upsilon Fraternity. He later went to the University of Seville in Spain to study art history and the works of Leonardo da Vinci.

Brown went into music and teaching, and almost gave up as a writer before moving up to write bestsellers. Some of his works include *Deception Point, Digital Fortress, Angels and Demons*, and *The Da Vinci Code*—a runaway bestseller that has sold more than 25 million copies in 2005 alone, and his latest novel, *The Lost Symbol.* What is the magic that has made him a millionaire author?

First, Brown is a plot master and is adept in the use of suspense.

Moreover, he researches his stories and marries facts with fiction.

Further to the above, the author knows what his audience wants. He has successfully tapped into the fears of readers who are searching for a secret key or missing mark that explains life.

He is married.

Bunyan, John

John Bunyan was born in 1628 at Elstow near Bedford, England, into a wealthy family that fell into bad times. The little-schooled writer was fond of *The King James Bible* while his contemporaries like John Milton and John Dryden immersed themselves in the classics.

He wrote about sixty controversial religious tracts and three fictional works. However, the "the village Rochester" also nicknamed "Bishop Bunyan" rode to fame after he wrote *The Pilgrim's Progress*, a religious allegory of his autobiographical work, *Grace Abounding to the Chief Sinners*. Incidentally, this masterful work, the most widely read book after the Bible, was written during his twelve years and six months' imprisonment at Bedford jail. It equally spawned Thackeray's novel, *Vanity Fair*—after

Vanity-Fair—a scene in the book. Why was it an echo-Bible?

Bunyan's language is simple and his readers could relate to the story. Also, the book is full of humor and the reader could not help laughing in most part of it. The characters have weaknesses like us and are either good or bad—people that live around us.

The book has greatly influenced the English language with the author's skillful naming of places and characters like Christian, Faithful, Hopeful, Worldly-Wiseman, Apollyon, Lord Hategood, Mr. Malice, Mr. Liar, Talkative, Great Heart (characters); Shadow of Death, Giant Despair, Vanity-Fair, Delectable Mountains, Doubting-Castle, Valley of Humiliation, the Slough of Despond, The Hill of Difficulty (places). It is no wonder that S.T. Coleridge said of the author: "His piety was baffled by his genius; and Bunyan the dreamer overcame the Bunyan of the conventicle."

The dreamer and genius died in 1688.

Christie, Agatha

Agatha Christie "the Queen of crime" was born of American and British parents on September 15, 1890 in Torquay in the country of Devon, England. She was educated by her mother after her father's death and was twice married.

She wrote 78 crime novels, 6 romance novels, and 19 plays under the pen name Mary Westmacott. Her works are now available in 103 languages with 2 billion copies sold and a gross yearly royalty of $3.7 million. Her works include the masterpiece, *The Murder of Rodger Ackrovd*, and her best play, *The Mousetrap*. Why did she write bestsellers?

She wrote on crime and love—topics that touch hearts and souls.

Her choice of words is hypnotic, making her books "unputdownable" as one scientist said.

She became the Dame of the British Empire in 1971 and died in 1976.

Clancy, Thomas Leo Jr.

The American writer, Tom Clancy, was born April 12, 1947 at Baltimore, US. He studied English, wrote many bestsellers, won million-dollar writing contracts, and had writers brand their works as titles written by him.

Some of his successful works, which have been turned into movies are *The Hunt for Red October, Patriot Games,* and *Clear and Present Danger*. Others are *The Bear and the Dragon*, and *The Sum of All Fears.*

Why was Clancy a great success story?

He was very descriptive, paid attention to details, and had good plots. Also he wrote on espionage—a best-selling topic any day.

The author who was twice married, died October 1, 2013.

Dickens, Charles

The literary czar, Charles Dickens, was born into a humble family in 1812. He was a victim of child labor and suffered the shame of having his father locked up for a year at the debtor's prison at Marhalsea. Dickens had little education, read books on his own and taught himself shorthand, which later prepared him as a reporter.

He, however, got instant recognition from all and sundry when he began publishing his writings in installments in *The Pickwick Papers*. Why was he considered the first Victorian novelist?

Dickens knew what his readers wanted. He could make them weep or laugh. His novels are humorous and satirical—readers enjoy reading such works.

The excitement in his novels arises from his picturesque descriptions and exaggerated characters. Some of his unforgettable characters are

Barkis (willing), Pegotty (undecided), Ebenezer Scrooge (miserly), Uriah Heep (umble), Mrs .Sarah Gamp (ever with her large cotton umbrella), and Mr. Michael Micawber (waiting for something to turn up).

Among his celebrated works are *The Old Curiosity Shop* (readers wept for dead Little Nell), *Oliver Twist* (he asked for more), *A Tale of Two Cities* (influenced by Thomas Carlyle's *French Revolution)*, and the autobiographical *David Copperfield* (Dickens' favorite).

He died in 1870.

James, E. L

E. L. James, whose real name is Erika Mitchell, was born March 7, 1963 in London, England, and educated at the University of Kent. She is the author of the trilogy, *Fifty Shades of Grey, Fifty Shades Darker,* and *Fifty Shades Freed.* The novels have topped bestseller lists, sold 100 million copies, been translated into 52 languages and adapted into movie. Why is the series a blockbuster?

Fifty Shades is an erotica romance work full of sex scenes, and sex literature sells.

The author is married with children.

Forsyth, Frederick

Frederick Forsyth, the British reporter turned novelist, was born August 25, 1938 in Ashford, Kent.

His best-known works are *The Day of the Jackal*, *The Dogs of War*, and *The Fist of God*. Others are *The Odessa File, Icon*, and *The Devil's Alternative*.

Why are his works blockbusters?

His stories are well researched, full of details, and very informative. He writes thrillers—stories of crime and spying—which is another advantage.

The author does not believe in the European dream.

Gogol, Nicholai Vasilevich (Ianovskii)

Nicholai Gogol, whose real surname was Ianovskii, was born in March 1809 at Sorotchinetz, in Little Russia—growing up in his parents' country estate. In that same year, literary greats such as Charles Darwin, Alfred Lord Tennyson, Abraham Lincoln, Edgar Poe, Gladstone, Holmes, Chopin, and Mendelssohn were also born.

Aleksandra Pushkin and Walter Scott influenced the educated Gogol in his writing. Considered the founder of the "critical realism" in Russian literature, his best work is *Dead Souls*—the surrealistic adventures of Pavel Ivanovich Chichikov, a merchant of dead souls. Some of his works include *The Robbers, The Inspector General, The Collected Tales of Nicholai Gogol, The Overcoat and Other Short Stories, Diary of a Madman and Other Stories.*

But why was Gogol successful as a writer? He was highly imaginative and had exceptional linguistic power. In his works, he exposed the defects of human character.

Later, under the influence of a fanatical priest, Father Konstantinovskii, Gogol burnt sequels for *Dead Souls*, became insane and died at Moscow on February 21, 1852. (Some say he was buried alive.) On his tomb was placed the old saying, "And I shall laugh with a bitter laugh." These were his last words.

He was married with children.

Goldsmith, Oliver

Oliver Goldsmith was born on November 10, 1730, in Ballymahon , Ireland . After his college education, he lived poor and wandered the continent.

Goldsmith conquered the three genres of literature with his masterpieces. These are *The Deserted Village*, a nostalgic poem on his desolate village; *She Stoops to Conquer*, a dramatic comedy based on his mistaken experience; and *The Vicar of Wakefield*, a great novel which he sold to pay his rent.

Goldsmith once boasted that anything his pen touches turns to gold. Why was he a literary loadstar?

His sentences sing letting the reader "see" and "feel" the actions in his story, and his use of suspense is beyond compare.

Oliver Goldsmith was a genius that puzzled his peers like Dr. Samuel Johnson, the wordsmith, who helped him sell the novel, and Horace Walpole who on account of the author's eccentricities gave him the mocking moniker, "inspired idiot."

.

The inspired idiot with the gold-turning pen was conquered by death on April 4, 1774.

Grisham, John

John Grisham was born in 1955 at Jonesboro, Arkansas, US. He studied law and accounting and was a politician.

First reluctant to go into writing, he came to write blockbusters which have been made into movies. They include *A Time to Kill, The Client, The Firm, The Chamber, The Rainmaker, The Street Lawyer*, among others.

Why does his books delight readers?

His writing style is simple and arresting.

He also tries to make his characters human and his narratives real.

In addition, Grisham is a plot master and tries to make his stories interesting.

The author is married with children.

Rowling, J.K

Joanne Kathleen Rowling was born July 31, 1965 in Chipping Sodbury, South Gloucestershire, England. She has a daughter from a failed marriage, lost her job, and was on the dole. But this single mother took the world by storm with her Harry Potter series—the story of a boy and his wizard kids in Hogwarts School of Witchcraft and Wizardry.

The author, who started writing at six, has Jane Austen as her favorite writer. She is the first dollar-billionaire writer and is richer than the Queen of England. Rowling has won international acclaim from her works, which have now been made into hit movies. Why did the books become runaway bestsellers?

First, she has a friendly subject—occult / paranormal—a topic that has captivated readers since *The Lord of the Rings* (J.R.R. Tolkien), *The Wizard of Oz* (L. Frank Baum), *Alice in Wonderland* (Lewis Carroll), and *The Narnia Chronicles* (C.S. Lewis).

Second, the books have wonderful plots and effective characters—loved and hated.

Third, her "humanization" of the witches and wizards who depart to school in a secret place at London's King's Cross Station (a real place), added plausibility to her story—something that other mystery writers haven't tried.

Last, the use of surprise (what happens in the next series?) also helped to turn the books to mega hits.

Because of the love for Harry Potter, the following phrases are becoming common place: Muggle (a non magical person), Quidditch (a wizard ball game played on brooms), Seeker (the best Quidditch player), Nimbus Two Thousand / Firebolt (names of activity brooms), The Sorting Hat (a school house cap), Parselmouth (a wizard who talks with snakes), Every Flavor Beans (a potpourri candy).

She lives with her daughter and second husband in Edinburgh, Scotland.

Rushdie, Salman

Salman Rushdie was born in Bombay (Mumbi) India on June 19, 1942 and educated in England. His first work was *Grimus* and his most controversial work, which earned him the fatwa, *Satanic Verses*, won him the Whitebread Award. His other works include *Midnight's Children, Shame, The Moor's Last Sigh, The Jaguar Smile, The Ground Beneath Her Feet* and *Shalimar The Clown*. Why did he write bestsellers?

He employs familiar backgrounds in his stories—myths, religion and folk tales. His narrative style of magical realism, which puts him in the likes of Angela Carter and Peter Carey among other writers, is a curious topic for readers.

His writing is full of charm, almost hypnotic. Books written in this way are arresting.

The author has won the Booker and was recently knighted.

He has married four times.

Tolstoy, Leo

Leo Tolstoy was born in the family estate of Yasnaya Polyana, in Tula Province, Russia September 9, 1828. He was a university dropout, lost his parents at childhood, became a drunk and gambler, and joined the army.

Tolstoy wrote several books but *War and Peace,* which has been dubbed the best novel of our time, was his greatest. Why did he write well?

His stories have good plots, effective characters, and simple style, and he was very descriptive.

His other masterpiece, *The Kreutzer Sonata,* which fictionalizes the love life of the author and his secretary-wife led to his excommunication.

He died November 20, 1910 and according to his will, was buried by a "green stick" that never was.

Wolfe, Tom

Tom Wolfe was born March 2, 1931, in Richmond, Virginia, U.S. He holds a Ph.D degree, and was a reporter before venturing into novel writing.

He has written many bestsellers which include *The Kandy-Kolored Tangerine-Flake Streamline Baby, The Electric Kool-Aid Acid Test, The Pump House Gang, The Painted Word, The Right Stuff, The Bonfire of the Vanities, A Man in Full, I Am Charlotte Simmons*, among others. *The Bonfire of the Vanities* earned $5 million for film rights—the highest by any author. What is the secret behind his success?

Wolfe is a hard working writer. He believes that his form of writing is the best for all America. Besides, he is creative, has good plots for his novels and possesses a good command of the English language.

He is married with two children.

What is common with the above bestselling authors?

First, they are novels / short stories, and fiction sells.

The second thing is that the authors wrote on subjects that they understood, knew their language, had good plots, and portrayed their characters well.

What then are the topics that sell?

CHAPTER 3

BESTSELLING TOPICS TO WRITE ON

"The best angler in the world will catch nothing if he throws his net in the Dead Sea."

—Irving Wardle

Who will read this story? That is the first question an author must consider before writing. It is unproductive to spend nights and days writing and re-writing only to release a work to an unreceptive public. Consider writing on a strange topic like The Dance of a Cockroach. Who cares? It is only a mental exercise to keep the writer on duty. But if you are writing for money (the muses forgive you), you must target an audience for your work.

Now, let's consider bestselling subjects to write about.

Love and sex stories make blockbusters

Any work on sex, love, and relationship is a wheel of fortune.

E .L. James is making money with her *Fifty Shades* trilogy because of the sex in the novels.

The film, *Love and Sex*, by Valerie Breiman got instant attention with hundreds turned back when it premiered at the Sundance Film Festival to a packed theater.

Works like these get both positive and negative reviews but that also helps to propel the sales. However, porn and erotic are to be avoided as most publishers and readers will not touch it.

Readers are looking for how-to books

People are looking for books that will teach them how to do things. Consider the following: how to become rich, how to cure diseases, how to make American dishes, how to build a house, how to drive a car, how to win a lady, how to write a story, the list is endless.

Success books are in great demand

Many people are looking for key to success in this world. For most of them, a motivational or inspirational book would suffice.

Writers like Anthony Robbins and Robert Kiyosaki have filled this need and become rich.

Mystery books are hot

Readers are interested in worlds or things that they do not see or know about. That explains why stories on extraterrestrials, witches, wizards, and so on are selling. And why J.K. Rowling became a billionaire just writing about witches and wizards in the *Harry Potter* series.

The Man Booker Prize judges have even popularized this genre, also called magical realism, by awarding the coveted prize to any that wrote on it: Salman Rushdie (*Midnight's Children*), Ben Okri (*The Famished Road*), and Arundhati Roy (*The God of Small Things*).

Controversial books make lunch tickets

If a work sparks debate, interest in the book will skyrocket. Why? Readers want to know what makes the work controversial.

Controversial works are easy to write. Sometimes, only a sentence or two is enough to generate the debate that is needed to sell a book. Ask Salman Rushdie, author of *Satanic Verses*.

Nevertheless, controversial works need not be scandalous, defamatory, libelous, or offensive.

Readers are looking for Doomsday Books

Yes, apocalyptic literature makes bestsellers any day. And disciples of Nostradamus are on hand to whet their appetite. Doomsday writers lined their pockets with cash writing about the end of the world at the dawn of the millennium. Yet, the world did not end.

However, interest in the final hour has not waned. There are always readers who are concerned about some wandering, earth-bound comet or last-day prophecy.

Spiritual Books are echo Bibles

Many people are now seeking spiritual help outside the Bible. This has created a new market for faith writers who are offering spiritual help to victims of child abuse, rape, broken marriages and the like. Among them is Iyanla Vanzant who wrote *Yesterday I Cried.*

Science Fiction has readership

Writers have dreamt better dreams about space and written books on it long before the space shuttles, *Spirit* and *Opportunity*, went to Mars and words started filtering out about the first human exodus to the red planet. There is so much to dream about the terrifying cosmos apart from ET's. So Science Fiction will always be a cash cow.

Thrillers excite readers

The increase in crime and espionage in this world gave rise to thrillers, writers who write them, secret agents who study the books and readers who love such works. Any thriller with a suspense will always be a must-read.

Fantasy titles make goodreads

Readers like to be taken to a Happy Valley or Fortunate Isles—away from the wars, terrorism, hunger, diseases, and deaths in this world—at least on the pages of a book. The writer therefore helps the reader to fantasize.

Parallel-world stories in demand

An irrational story that reverses historical facts can entice readers. Philip K. Dick did it with *The Man in the High Castle* where he wrote that the Allies were the losers of the Second World War. And Philip Roth's *The Plot Against America* made it to the bestsellers' list with fascism in America.

Now, where do you source the materials for your story?

CHAPTER 4

WHERE TO SOURCE YOUR MATERIALS

"Writing is thinking, and thinking is work."

--Robert Bolt

Now, did you know how Mary Shelley came to write *Frankenstein*? She was vacationing in Switzerland with her husband, Percy Bysshe Shelley, the poet Lord Byron and another named Polidori. After familiarizing themselves with ghost stories, Lord Byron came up with the proposition: "We will each write a ghost story."

Then each went to dream dreams, and Mary Shelley thought that in order to excel, she would have to dream up the scariest story ever. And she beat them all with *Frankenstein*, the weirdest story before Harry Potter.

However, imagination comes from sources and the writer would benefit from the following:

Reading

An aspiring author must be a voracious reader. Read for pleasure or on purpose anything that interests you: newspapers, magazines, story and scientific books.

If you are planning to write a book on science fiction, for instance, read books on the subject.

As you read, ask yourself: *What is the writer saying? Why is he saying it? Where did this story take place? How is he saying it?* The answers you get will help you comprehend and appreciate the book.

Observation

Now, come to think of it. Which invention was ever made without a keen observation: from Isaac Newton observing a falling apple (gravity) to Archimedes jumping out of a pool of water and solving the riddle of the king's crown (Eureka!).

So, in your daily activities, make it a habit to observe closely; who knows, right in your garden, you might discover the remains of an extinct dinosaur! That was how Daniel Dafoe stumbled on source material to write the novel *Robinson Crusoe*. While in hiding during the French revolution, he found an inscription of an actual account on Alexander Sykll, a castaway. He then fictionalized on it to write his blockbuster, changing the name of the marooned hero to Man Friday.

Personal experiences

Who was it that said experience is the best teacher? He was probably right.

People have written masterpieces and autobiographies based on their life experiences. Consider Charles Darwin (*On The Origin of Species*), Nelson Mandela (*Born to Run*), Wole Soyinka (*The Man Died*), and Hillary Clinton (*Hard Choices*).

Investigation

The writer must have an inquiring, probing mind. Socrates, the great philosopher, asked to know. Ask published writers to tell you their experiences. Some writers travel long distances to collect materials for their story.

However, the Web and libraries are also available. They can be good research tools if the author knows what they want and how to search for information.

CHAPTER 4

HOW TO ENTITLE YOUR WORK

"The world of books is the most remarkable creation of man."—Clarence Day

How you entitle your story is important because it is your best chance to invite a reader to take a second look. How do you then get a good title for your book?

Your title must reflect the subject of your book. You should therefore guard against writing a misleading title.

To choose a title is very easy. After you have gotten your subject area, narrow it to a topic suitable for your writing.

Let's take cloning for example. That's a wide subject. Now, break it down into topics, and you will have a list that reads like this: Origin, types, advantages, disadvantages, and so on. Now, how do you entitle your book?

First, your title should be short. You may use a word (*Coriolanus*) by William Shakespeare, a phrase (*A Tale of Two Cities*) by Charles Dickens or a sentence (*The Beautiful Ones Are Not Yet Born*) by Ayi Kwei Armah.

If the title becomes so long that it cannot be remembered by your reader or be read at a glance, it loses its purpose. A title might even be framed like a question, *What's Wrong with Cloning?*

Second, you may give your book a subtitle for effect, or to enable a better understanding of the book. For instance: *Twelfth Night; or What You Will* by William Shakespeare. Beware that your subtitle does not conflict with your major title. That will spell doom for the book from the beginning. So, if you are unsure of a subtitle, leave it out.

Third, your title should be catching and attractive. This may require a great deal of thinking. But it is worth the effort. The title of your book should be able to tell a reader that they have something to gain from reading the book. Think of the title of this book you are reading. Who wouldn't like to write a bestseller?

Fourth, your title should be in good taste. Consider: *The Gospel According to Satan.* I don't think many readers would like to touch that with a ten-foot pole.

Fifth, do not give serial title. Certain writers stamp the same title on all their books. It may suit such writers but not their readers who may find it difficult to tell the old from the new. It may help when you are writing in episodes like the series on Harry Potter.

Sixth, be ready to change your book title if it is not convenient or if it is not helping the book sales. Such timely actions by writers have helped to save their books.

Now, it has been said that giving your book a title at first would be a good start. This will help you in your research and guide you in the development of your bestseller.

On the other hand, some tested writers finish their work before choosing a title. Which one do you like?

While you think about that, let us discuss another small matter.

What Name Should I Use?

Of course, you have a name. Use your legal name to write your book. Or would you want to use a pen name? Well, it doesn't matter.

Some writers though are seized by the superstition that names sell books. Well, if you have written good books before, that may be true.

Otherwise, it may not be necessary for you to worry about it.

Be that as it may, you may decide to do any of the following: Use your real name (*Weep Not Child* by James Ngugi), anglicize your names (*Heart of Darkness* by Joseph Conrad from Joseph Konrad), use a pseudonym (*Animal Farm* by George Orwell—real name Eric Blair), shorten your name (*Things Fall Apart* by Chinua Achebe, from Chinualumogu Achebe), or imitate the great Greek writers (*Odyssey* by Homer—single name), what is his second name?

But is the actual writing process as easy as you think?

CHAPTER 5

WRITING IN PRACTICE

"Writing is thinking, not thinking about thinking."—Robert Bolt

Writing the first sentence in a story is scarier than an ogre. It is not surprising therefore that authors have unfinished stories. What are some of the impediments?

The beginning and end of the story

Some beginners spend months on end wondering how to start and end their story. When they finally begin, they are at a loss as to how to develop the story. And if they pull that out, the next question will be, How do I end the story?

You do not approach story writing as if you were about to sit for your final exam in college. The idea will not come because you are not in your natural frame of mind.

You begin writing your story when you are relaxed. Consider it as fun. If this still worries you, tell your story to a friend and have it recorded. Then transcribe it and have it edited. That's it!

Writer's block

Yet, you may even find yourself unable to write because of what is called writer's block. What causes it?

The first cause is you. If you are seized by fear, are sick or have psychological problems, the muse will fail you. That is why you should be in your best frame of mind to write a story.

The second is external. The people around you—your friends and close relatives—could discourage you by telling you that you are merely wasting your time. You may even be denied access to research materials. One writer had his books burnt while another was imprisoned in a dark room by "sympathetic" relatives who wrongly thought that the writer was going crazy!

The environment can also be a factor. A noisy or polluted environment can hamper writing. Why not then look for a conducive place to write?

Length of story

How long will a story be? You should not be overly concerned with the length of the book. The bestsellers are not the most voluminous books. It is the message of a story that sells it, not the volume.

Let's consider some titles. The *Old Man and the Sea* by Ernest Hemingway, *Animal Farm* by George Orwell and *The Lord of the Flies* by William Golding were great books in their time and are still selling today. But they are not voluminous titles.. Rudyard Kipling and H.G. Wells are best remembered for their short stories.

Never let a publisher ruin your book by insisting that you lengthen your story when it has already ended. Friends can also spoil your story in that way. But the wise course is never to continue dragging a story that has stopped. There will be looseness in the construction and a good reader will find out that you are just filling in irrelevant materials. Like a vehicle out of gas, it stops!

What style should I write?

When you start thinking of how to style your story so as to make you the best stylist that the world has ever had, you will not begin your story. The fact is: You are your style and the more you write, the more your style matures.

For example, James Joyce and Virginia Woolf perfected the stream of consciousness technique, a style that employs their character's flow of thought and feeling to tell their story instead of using the traditional descriptive method. Why not invent your style?

The strange case of Bertold Brecht, the poet and writer, underscores the futility of striving for the quintessential style. He wrote well, and writers wanted to learn his style. But what Bertold taught them was not what he wrote, and what his disciples taught others was not what the master taught. That is the strange thing about Brecht—and style.

Duration of writing

It is better to spend enough time writing your book before getting it published. Readers recognize a mature and a hurried work. It is only news media people that work on deadlines. Your book should not be written in haste.

It took J.K. Rowling 7 years to write the first Harry Potter and 4 fruitless years searching for a publisher. William Golding wrote *The Lord of the Flies* in 10 years, and when he was ready to publish, everyone rejected it. It took the master storyteller Tom Wolfe 11 long years to write the commercial blockbuster *A Man in Full*. And Mark Twain, the celebrated American writer and humorist, labored 25 years on his autobiography—writing some 44 drafts of the same book!

Research

It can be unnerving to find research materials for a work. It might seem that there are a lot of materials in our today's world. But sometimes the material that you are looking for may neither be in the library nor on the Internet. It could be in your backyard!

Were you wondering why it took Tom Wolfe 11 years to write *A Man in Full*? He had to leave the United States and embark on a world tour to get his materials—even going to Russia. But in the end, what he was looking for was in America!

And Dan Brown left America in search of content for his book. He found source for *The Da Vinci Code* in a church in Scotland.

This can be pretty expensive for the beginning writer. Some hire researchers to scout for materials for their work. The pre-published author cannot afford this either.

In the end, it seems that the only sources of information for them are the ones discussed earlier in this book—reading, observation, personal experiences, interviewing people, and of course, imagination.

Peer Review

One thing that you will like to take advantage of is peer review. You and a few friends who are writers might form a literary group for the purpose of reading, previewing, and critiquing one another's work.

This early phase of criticism will help you in improving on your first and subsequent drafts. But know this: criticisms should be objective. And no matter what your friends say, there is no substitute for professional touch.

Now, how do you introduce and end your story?

CHAPTER 6

HOW TO BEGIN AND END A STORY

"Let your opening be glorious, your finishing spectacular. That way no one would mind your flaws in-between."—Author unknown

It is good to begin a story gloriously and end it in a spectacular way. However, before you start writing a story, it would be a good thing to develop an outline.

The Outline

Since you have a topic and a diary full of notes, making an outline won't be difficult. This is the time for you to select and put down the materials you want to use. The title of your book, which you have already chosen, will help you to determine what comes in, or goes out.

You may start by writing a brief storyline. Then make a list of your characters including what each of them will do in your story. After that, write the main points of your story, which will later become chapters, and put the sub-points under them.

Some characters would appear in more than one chapter and an action started in an earlier chapter might continue unfolding in later chapters. Indicate this in your outline as well.

As you progress in shaping your outline, ask yourself these questions: *Do the main points point to the title of my book? Are all my main points distributed according to the chapters? Do the subpoints support the development of actions in each chapter? Can I develop each entry satisfactorily? Does the presentation follow the order of my story?*

If the answers you get are positive, it means that you have crossed the Rubicon. But if not, you have to re-work your outline.

The outline is like shifting sands driven here and there by the wind before forming a beautiful sand dune by the sea or desert.

You can therefore keep adjusting your outline as you develop your story. Some experienced writers, however, do not write with an outline. They have the story in their head!

Now you know that you have to introduce your story. This is the first point in your outline.

In story writing, you have to tantalize your reader, you have to make them keep holding on to your book.

Making a Good Introduction

A good introduction must have three ingredients.

First, it must arouse the interest of your readers. This means that you must have the power to hook them right from the start. Keep them in a perpetual state of expectation. Let them keep saying to themselves: "I am damned, if I don't read this!"

Second, your introduction must have bearing to the topic of your writing. Otherwise, your reader will lose you.

There must therefore be a bridge from your introduction, which will link your main story. Let them know where you are taking them through in the journey. But do not allow them to be too familiar with the terrain: You would have concluded the story before it began! Give some, keep some. Let them see the shadow, but keep the substance.

Third, your introduction must have appropriate length. What is proper depends on some other factors, such as the length of the book. Consider a book whose introduction is longer than the story.

It is, therefore, left for you to determine how long or how short your introduction should be. But note this: It should not be too short that you sacrifice your reader's interest and the purpose of your writing. And it should not be too long that your reader starts wondering when the actual story would begin.

How to end a Story

There are no rules. But let your reader know that the story has actually ended. Many would heave a sigh of relief and have a good laugh.

On the other hand, you may decide not to "end" the story Put the reader in suspense and let them imagine the end. By then most actions in the story would have been resolved so that it would be an easy guess. Some writers prefer this style.

Now, let's go to the heart of the matter—the story.

CHAPTER 7

HOW TO DEVELOP YOUR STORY

*"Imagination is better than knowledge."—Albert
Einstein*

You are not new in the art of storytelling because
you have had cause to tell friends or relatives of
experiences or incidents that you may have seen or
heard—at home, work, school, or while in transit.

It is the same way you use to narrate such incidents
that you are to use to construct your story—straight,
from the heart.

Suppose you witnessed a street fight. How you
narrate what happened to your friends is the same
way you put it down in writing—including your
exclamations, regressions, and humor.

Let's say a dozen persons witnessed this incident.
Do you know that if these twelve people were asked
to say what happened that each one would present
their story in their own way?

One may pay more attention to the fighters, another
one would be more interested in the antics of the
onlookers, and the other may be more concerned
with the side attraction—the pickpockets. But the
subject matter is the same—a fight scene.

Now, if this incident becomes a matter for a story competition, and there is going to be a prize for the best writer, how would you present your story so as to win the first prize?

You are now going to fall back on your imagination.

The following will help you to get right this thing called plot. Ask yourself these questions:

How do I begin?

This is why you should have a good introduction because it is the background to the structure of your story.

You are to explain the background of your story to your reader. Or, you may use your characters to do it.

Where does this story take place?

This is the location or setting of your work. You may decide to use real or imaginary places, depending on its nature. You may also use several settings. Time periods for the events are also important.

Who are the characters?

These are the people in the story. You, the writer, determines their roles and fate.

What is the heart of the matter?

This is the major conflict of your story. It must be clearly defined, and the actions have to revolve around it. For example, is it a conflict between a man and himself, his "destiny," or nature? Or is it a conflict between individuals? And it must be carefully guarded so that your reader does not pre-empt the outcome of the story.

How do I develop the action?

You may have to build a rising action in which one force gains control over the other and a falling action whereby the opposite happens. Of course, this is made possible by the characters and the conflicts in your story.

What about the climax?

You could situate the climax (the most important or exciting event) half-way around your story, followed with the anticlimax (the uneventful part), toward the end.

How will I end the story?

This is called the denouement and this stage is very important. Your reader should know that things have been sorted out and that your story has actually ended. If they do not recognize this, you have failed.

Now that you have gotten your story going, let us look more closely at the people that will help in the movement of your story—the characters.

CHAPTER 8

THE CHARACTERS IN YOUR STORY

*"The world wants to be deceived."—Sabastian
Brant*

If art is a reflection of life, then there should be
people in your story because in life people make
history, either for good, or for bad.

It is just as easy to create characters in a story. Just
look around you, and you will find them.

So, using your sources you may have developed
some characters for your story.

Types of Characters

The characters in your story may be persons or
animals. You will have the hero / heroine playing
the major part and others playing minor parts in the
story.

We have the following types of characters:

Two-dimensional characters

These do not look like real people. Jonathan Swift used them in Gulliver's Travels.

Three-dimensional characters

These are true-life people having good qualities and character flaws. You will find some in the works of Joseph Conrad.

The following questions will help you to make effective characterization.

Who should be a character?

That depends on the nature of your story. Anything could be a character. In the Bible, a snake and a donkey spoke, and trees were characters in a Bible mock drama.

So, your characters may be humans (*David Copperfield* by Charles Dickens), witches (*Macbeth* by William Shakespeare), animals (*Animal Farm* by George Orwell).

How should they be named?

First, their names should not be too long and foreign that your reader finds them difficult to remember.

Second, use revealing titles like Dr. and Prof., King and Queen, to help your reader grasp them easily. Historical names are beyond compare in this regard.

Third, the names of your characters may be used to provide clues to their quality like Christian and Morality in *The Pilgrims' Progress*.

How many should they be?

They should not be too many if you don't want to confuse your reader. The principal characters should stand clear from the minor ones.

Are my characters believable?

If you start by wondering whether your reader may believe your characters or not, you will not excel. Your reader may identify with one or two of your characters. The characters in Charles Dickens' stories are unbelievable.

How should they speak?

You will have to vary the speech patterns of your characters. From the royal and dignified speech of a king to the learned and pedantic discourse of scientists; from the lowly and untrained language of a court servant to the meaningless quibbling of a child.

In short, the speeches should reflect the various social, cultural, and educational backgrounds of your characters.

What are my characters' motives?

There should be a motive for the actions of your characters. If your reader doesn't find satisfactory motives behind the actions of your characters, then you have not written well.

Do my characters contribute to the development of my story?

In story writing, you may decide to be the storyteller, or you may leave that task to one or several of your characters.

What your characters say therefore should have bearing to the subject matter and the outworking of your story. Put differently, they should do the work you want them done.

Do you want them to fight over something, or to love or kill themselves? Which character is doing what, and which characters are in the know, or are ignorant of those actions?

In doing so, you are using your characters to inform your reader. And if you do it well, you would have succeeded in pulling out a good story.

CHAPTER 9

YOUR LANGUAGE AND STYLE

"Proper words in proper places make the true definition of a style."—Jonathan Swift

Beginning writers worry about style. But what is style? A writer says: "Style is the man himself." You are what you write! That means you are a unique person, and your style should also be unique. Do not therefore start by aping another writer's style.

Now, let's consider a few things about the language and style of your work.

Sentence Structure

This is important because your story will be written in sentences. Your sentences should support your theme. They should say what you mean.

It will also be nice to vary your sentence patterns. Mix short and long sentences, but not too long that your reader finds himself gasping for breath. There should be no too much fancy expressions, or affected constructions.

There should be unity in your sentence structure and a smooth transition from one paragraph to the other.

The active voice, (It is interesting) is preferred to the passive voice, (It is being interesting).

Diction

Your choice of words and phrases matters. The beginning writer should not use high sounding, impressive words. Try simple expressions. Shun abstract diction and formulaic terms like clichés and jargons.

Instead, use concrete language. Say, "The boy who stole my pen," not "The expropriator of my calligraphic material."

Tone

The tone of your work should be personal and friendly. Yes, the informal style is recommended as opposed to the formal and impersonal tone. Refer to yourself as "I." Address your reader as "you." Use "we" or "us" to refer to your reader and yourself.

So, use the tone that you would use to speak to your friend but do not be too informal or slangy. However, you should use appropriate tone for your characters—formal, semi-formal, informal, colloquial, and slang—depending on their educational background.

Also, avoid offensive languages such as racist overtones. Remember that you intend your work to be read by all nations, tribes, peoples, tongues, different age groups, and by both sexes. If then the tone of your work is biased, you would lose readership.

Distance

It is not the language that you use as a doctor in a seminar of the College of Surgeons or as a scientist in a space ship full of astronauts that you use when talking to the common man. The tone of your language therefore dictates the distance between you and your reader.

If the distance is far, your reader may feel you don't consider him; and put your book away. But if the distance is close, he will be happy to read on.

Figures of Speech

Figures of speech or imagery should be used with care as they tend to be abstract, but when carefully used, they enhance the beauty of your language.

You do not need to read a book of figures of speech to know them because it is part of our daily expressions.

If you therefore write the way you speak, your peculiar language and style will be manifest.

CHAPTER 10

HOW TO REVISE YOUR BOOK

"The time to begin writing an article is when you have finished it to your satisfaction."

—Mark Twain

Revising actually means writing and re-writing. If you choose to revise your book, the following questions under the appropriate sub-headings will help you in your revision:

Subject Revision

Do I have an interesting subject matter?

This means having a topic that will interest your readers. In the process of revising, you do well to ask yourself if your story is really a good read.

Some have tried to cut through the demographic divide in their book. Others try to appeal to both male and female readers. Still some writers try to reach the "pop corn crowd"—the young and the old. Other writers go for the "edgy content" by providing large dose of violence, sex, and crime scenes in their works (something for everyone).

Is my subject matter thoroughly handled?

Evaluate the language and tone of your work, your characterization and dialogue, the development and resolution of the story, and see if they helped the subject of your story. .

Have I satisfactorily handled objections that may arise from my story?

There can be no better way of handling objections in a work than by addressing them in the book. For example, if you wrote that there is a human civilization under the sea, the best way to disarm your critics is perhaps by making one of your characters mock those who think that man cannot live under the sea.

Does the title of my book suit my story?

It would be a terrible thing if what you wrote does not match the title of your work. That is why some title their work before they begin writing and keep it in focus through the duration of the writing. Of course, if you notice that the title is inappropriate, change it!

Can my readers believe it?

Whether you are writing fiction or non-fiction, you should make your story believable. That is the purpose of creative writing. Even if the story is out of this world, make the reader enjoy it.

Do I expect them to believe?

You would not necessarily begin a story wondering whether your readers would believe it or not. People read sci-fi and mystery books and "deceive" themselves into believing the stories.

The way you handle your subject matter determines this.

Structural Revision

Do my main points stand out?

One way you can make the main point of your work to stand out is by repetition. You can do this by the use of illustration, reasoning, and demonstration. If you read your book without understanding the major points of your work, you have not done well.

Do the sub points support the main points?

Check to see if you have provided enough support for the ground of your story. Do you need to do more research? Remembering that there can be no effect without cause will help you to know if there is a gap in the story

*Is there unity from my introduction to the
conclusion?*

If there is a looseness of construction in your story,
then there is disharmony in your work. This should
not surprise you as it occurs in early drafts—
particularly in the writings of beginners. Check the
weak spots and make them stick.

*Are my facts sufficient, or do I need further
supporting materials?*

It can be tedious and time wasting to research a
story but that's a bit easy with the Web.

Your description of a people's culture should be
accurate even if they are far apart as the poles—
from the bush Maori tribe of New Zealand to the
Mosuo people on the shores of Lugu Lake in China,
where men and women do not marry and where
there is no family life!

*Do my characters work out my purpose for the
story?*

Let's say you have terrorists and anti-terrorist
agents in your story. Did you intend the terrorists to
be caught in the course of mailing a bomb or not?
That is a great part of your story that you should not
overlook.

Is my conclusion appropriate?

Did you intend your story to end as a tragedy, comedy, tragic-comedy, suspense, or some other form? Then you have to find out if it was so.

Grammatical Revision

Have I conformed to the standard rules of English grammar?

See if you got the following right: subject-verb agreement, pronoun reference, use of modifiers, idioms, collocations, and so on.

Are my spellings and punctuation correct?

First, ask yourself whether you are writing American, or British, English because there is difference between the two forms in spelling, punctuation, and usage. Even in American English, there are variations. Whichever form you use, be consistent.

Did I write what I meant?

This calls for preciseness in your use of the language. As much as possible, avoid redundancies and circumlocution. Of all the things that readers hate, these are the foremost. When a writer begins to say things over and over again, the reader feels that he has nothing new to say—just filling pages, and wasting their time!

Are my sentences and paragraphs correct and harmonious?

Your sentences should be fully developed into paragraphs, which are in turn joined by transitional connectives—no matter whether you use direct, pivoting, or suspended, paragraphs.

Have I used appropriate tone?

The language of the characters in your book should not be the same. You could mix formal, informal, colloquial, or slang, but what is the overriding tone of the work?

Do the speeches of my characters match their roles in the story?

Did the king or clown in your story play their part well? Did they speak monologues or dialogues? Were their speeches ironical, sarcastic, or comical? The answers to these questions will help you in the reporting and movement of your story.

Of the three forms of revision listed above, the last—grammatical editing—which the editors like to call editing or polishing, is the most difficult, especially for non-native speakers of the language. You would therefore have to trouble-shoot to master it.

You can have your work critiqued and edited by a sympathetic professional. Try these sites:

http://www.pred-ed.com

http://www.writersedgeservice.com

However, there are things you must know before publishing your book.

CHAPTER 11

MANUSCRIPT EVALUATION

"Criticism is easy, art is difficult."—French author.

After the final revision of your manuscript, it would be helpful to request a professional to give you a diagnostic review of your work. The reviewer will look at all or some of the following:

Title suitability

The title of the work has to have bearing with the storyline. If the plot differs with the book title, then there is a disconnection.

The reviewer would like to know if the author developed the plot along the title of the story.

Genre requirement

The story would have to match a genre, though sometimes the genres overlap. But the overriding category of the story would have to be clear to the reviewer.

Some critics would look for similarity with a published work. If they find one, they would like to know if it is original and whether it can compete against the already published book.

Book audience

Who will read this story? is the question that the evaluator would like to know. They want to know if the work has a narrow or wide readership and whether the audience is defined.

Of course, this leads to one thing: marketability. If the work has market, then there is prospect for it upon publication.

Story length

The reviewer would also like to know if the work under review meets the book length requirement, and whether the writer understands this. The length of a book, however, is dependent on the author, the genre, publisher, or association.

The standard requirement for a novel is 80,000-100,000 words, though there have been classics like *Animal Farm* (30,000 words) and *War and Peace* (500,000 words).

The Science Fiction and Fantasy Writers of America recommends the following:

Novel.... over 40,000 words

Novella.... 17,500-40,000 words

Novelette.... 7,500-17,500 words

Short story under.... 7, 500 words

Characters

The reviewer likes to know whether the characters are real and have thoughts and feelings like the real people that they represent.

On the other hand, are they lifeless, stereotypical characters? The reader is not able to relate with such characters in a story as they would to the real characters.

Plot

The story has to be interesting, engaging, and believable. The writer crafts the story in any way that would entice the reader to find out more.

If the reviewer finds the story development uninspiring and epileptic, then the writer would expect some hard knocks.

Pace and Structure

The reviewer wants to know if it is a fast-moving story without unnecessary trivialities.

On the other hand, it should not be a dull story with no actions. And the story should not be too fast-spaced that the reader fails to grasp the theme. A long story may start slow and move faster as the plot unfolds.

Command of Language

There is nothing like reading a work written in perfect English with the vocabulary, imagery, and figures of speech in the right places. It helps in the comprehension of the story, elevates the work, and adds to its enjoyment.

The reviewer will tell the author if the language was adequate or if it needs polishing.

Narrative Style

The evaluator would like to know if the writer's voice is original and matches the characters and tone of the narrative.

A colorless mimicking style would not advance the movement of the story.

Dialogue

The characters would have to talk to each other. They have to talk like real people and their conversation should help the reader to understand the characters and the story.

Conversely, a story where the characters make contrived speeches addressed to the reader is a failure.

Settings

The settings of the story should be clear to the reader; it governs the narrative zeitgeist.

If a work's setting is unclear, it would impact negatively on the narrative mood.

Subject matter and Ideas

The theme of the story should be vividly clear. The subject matter may incite the gray matter of the readers of the story.

A purposeless story that leaves the reader dumber after reading it will definitely make the writer get a spanking from the critics.

A comprehensive manuscript evaluation would assist you in discovering the weak and strong arears of your manuscript and determine whether you would need to revise the document before approaching a publisher.

Get free feedback/Peer Review

You can get a free critique of your work from fellow authors and even get your book noticed by agents. Try these sites:

http://www.authonomy.com

http://www.youwriteon.com

Showcase your Manuscript

You can pay and showcase your manuscript below:

http://www.authorlink.com

http://www.writersedgeservice.com

http://www.christianmanuscriptssubmission.com

QUESTION 12

QUESTIONS TO ASK BEFORE PUBLISHING A BOOK

"Publishing is a very mysterious business. It is hard to predict what kind of sale or reception a book will have."—Tom Wolfe

Publishing is an uncertain business. Before you send your work to the publisher therefore you will do well to ask yourself these questions:

Am I ready to gamble with the publishing cost?

To begin with, know this: book publishing is not cheap.

When we talk of publishing, however, we do not mean only the set up fee for producing your book. Other things are involved. To publish a good work, you would have to edit it before approaching the book publisher, and you should be prepared to market your work.

Then ask yourself: *Do I have this amount? Will it make a hole in my pocket? Can I risk the fee? Can I borrow it? If I do, will I be able to repay the loan?* These questions are appropriate so that you don't end up in the hole, or worse, bankruptcy.

74

You should know this: lack of fund seems to be the major problem of first-time writers.

Do I believe that people will read my book?

This question is very important because if you are not sure that anyone will pick your work, you have no business publishing it.

So you must have faith that your book will find an audience, even if it might not be a large one. For example, could your work be enjoyed by only a few friends or townsfolk, work or school mates? If so, you've got readers.

Is my theme such a timely and interesting one that the public should know?

It could be that the subject of your work is so timely that you can't wait. Could it be that the work is following an incident like a natural disaster such as an earthquake or a mine collapse, or a social problem like a terrorist attack or a revolution? Then it is the right time to publish your book!

In that case, it will be appropriate for you to find out from your publisher how long it will take for the publication. Some take days or weeks. For others it could be months. Can you afford the wait?

Is this the best market to publish my book?

Ordinarily, your locality is the best place to publish your work. But you have to ask yourself: *Will my folks read my book? Do they read books at all?*

Although the reading culture is dropping, if you feel that people in your land do not read books or if they are too poor to buy one, then you have a problem publishing where you live. Why not then publish your book where an average number of people can afford to buy and read books?

Modern technology has, however, made it possible for a book to be published anywhere and be read in hamlets around the earth.

If your work is published and made available to be downloaded in online bookstores on the Web, then you never need to worry whether you published in your home country or not. The important thing is availability!

Am I expecting responses from my readers?

Know that readers must react to your story. This is even more so if you have written a good book. Some critics might write to say that it was a good read while others might just say that it was the worst book that they have ever read.

This should neither surprise nor annoy you. After all, you need reader's response, and sometimes these comments help to pop up your book's sales.

Your other consolation is that these critics can't write or are afraid to write. You are a step ahead of them because you have written a book.

And know this: that perfect book that they are all looking for does not exist. It has not been written because man—the writer—is an imperfect creature.

Therefore be comforted with the words of the French author, Destouches: "Criticism is easy, art is difficult."

Will I benefit in one way or the other from the publication of this book?

A book's publication brings some measure of prestige and authority to the writer. It could help you to advance in your job, business, or career. It could widen your circle of associates. And your speaking travels could take you to foreign lands— places that you likely wouldn't have been. Would you like to take advantage of all these by publishing your book?

Will I be content even if I don't make money?

Consider this question closely because the mere fact that you have just published a book is not the equivalent of digging a field laid with gold. Truth is, It could make you poorer!

I will like to leave you with a home truth about book publishing: book publishers are not generally interested in book promotion. When you pay a publisher to publish your book, he has made all his profit. Period. The money he gets from the sales of your book only adds to his profit margin. His next move is to woo you to submit another work or to purchase a promotional package. And he makes more money.

It does not matter if the publishing fee is small. The publisher collects several other books from other authors. So the "small" profit he gets from each writer translates into huge sum of money.

Some authors are not able to recoup their publishing costs. So, is it okay with you if you don't sell a dime?

Is my publisher reliable?

The first thing to do when you begin thinking of publishing is to search for a reliable publisher. Choose a couple of names and send a query. You will find out that only half of them will reply, and out of that number only one will eventually play ball. Don't be surprised if one of them says that your poetry collection was the best thriller he has ever read but that the genre is not presently suitable for publication. Nor should it be a thing of wonder if you were to see your rejected book modified and published by another writer.

In selecting a publisher for your book, know that the "big" names are not necessarily the best. What matters is whether you will make money from the sales of your book, not who published it.

The greatest books were not published by the big publishing houses but by obscure printing houses, which saw great works, took a chance and later became famous.

John Bell became known after publishing Thomas Paine's *Common Sense*—a masterpiece that was rejected in 1776 by several publishers in Philadelphia. The book became the first American bestseller, selling 100,000 copies in ten weeks!

Canongate, the independent publisher of Yann Martel's *The Life of Pi* was voted Publisher of the Year after the book won the Man Booker Prize in 2002. So do not mind the name, but choose a publisher that performs.

Your success depends to a large extent on the integrity of your publisher. I should tell you that many of them are folding and ending up in endless lawsuits with their authors. The publishers that you knew some years ago are no more.

So before you send your book to a publisher, it would be wise for you to find out the following: Does the publisher give me the full copyright of my work? If he is editing my book, will he do a good job? Does the publisher pay a good royalty and is the payment prompt? Is he interested in promoting my book? Does he reply promptly to mails?

Can I promote my book?

Many people think that writing is difficult and that promotion is as easy as sipping a cup of tea. If you are in that number, you have put the cart and the horse in the wrong order because writing is a very sweet thing to do, but promotion is not a circus show.

In promotion, the buck stops at your table. You must be ready to promote your book. It is no other person's business than yours. It is your life!

The publisher might make your book available in all the search engines and bookstores around the globe but know that Web presence or publicity alone will not make your book sell. It might be that it is only your publisher and your circle of friends that know your book is out there. Meanwhile, your book is not selling. You only published and became a has-been—has been published. Is that good for you?

About 2 million books are published worldwide yearly and out of that number some 300,000 are published in the US. How can you therefore make the world know about your book out of the 2 million? So you see that it's a Sisyphean affair. If you are prepared to market your book, then it will go places!

Will I write again or is my writing just a flash in the pan?

When some authors publish a book that refuses to sell, they hang their pen in the attic. Will that be the case with you?

When the Bostonian, Edgar Allan Poe, self-published his poetry collection, *Tamerlaine and Other Poems* in 1827, only a few copies were sold. But do you know the price of a first edition copy of the book now? Twenty thousand dollars!

And now enter J. K. Rowling. When the unknown single mother wrote *Harry Potter and the Sorcerer's Stone* in 1997, she didn't get much notice. Several years after, her titles are now household names and the writer is sitting pretty today in a medieval castle in Edinburgh, Scotland.

The point then is, Would you continue writing if your first book fails, or would you chicken out?

Now look at the above questions again. How did you answer? If you answer "yes" to 5 or more of the above questions, I will advise you to seriously consider publishing your book. And success will attend you!

You may do the following before scouting for a publisher:

Copyright your Manuscript

Although your work has automatic copyright, you can give it additional protection by obtaining a copyright for it. Do it online below:

http://www.copyright.gov

http://www.ipo.gov

Get an ISBN

The International Serial Book Number is the 13-digit unique number for identifying your published book. This is not needed before you submit your work to an agent neither is it required if you are publishing an e-book. But an ISBN is compulsory if you are doing a paperback. You can get it below:

http://www.isbn.org

Some publishers can assign your book an ISBN.

Publishers, Agents, Query Letter Information

To get more details with regard to the above, go to:

http://www.agentquery.com

http://www.querytracker.com

http://www.publishersmarketplace.com

http://www.pred-ed.com

CHAPTER 13

WHERE TO PUBLISH YOUR BOOK

*"If you write without getting published, then there
is no use in writing at all."*

—Aldous Huxley

The following platforms are available for the author
to publish their books.

Trade Publishers

Also called commercial, or royalty, publishers,
these are the big fish in the publishing industry.
They include Longman, Macmillan, Heinemann,
Random House, Houghton Mifflin, Doubleday
Books, Little Brown and Co., and Brace
Jovanovich, among others. When you publish with
a royalty publisher, you forfeit control over content,
and price, and of course you will have no financial
obligations. You will however get an advance
payment of 10 percent to 15 percent thereafter.

The upfront payment and the pay-no-fees for
publishing may be attractive. But my advice to you
is that if you are pre-published, if you are a new
writer; do not waste your time submitting your
books to these "elephants." Because they will not
publish you!

Yes, they have published a few unknowns like Eric Segal (*Love Story*) and Kathleen Winsor (*Forever Amber*). But what about the countless others who got the polite rejection slip after twelve calendar months that reads: "We are sorry your book does not meet our present needs. Good luck."

So the point is that they don't have the time to read your book. Or they can't recognize a good book if they see one. Or they can't afford to risk their money publishing a new comer like you, without hope of getting huge profits. Or, all of the above.

But consider: If you were a great writer, perhaps a Nobel Laureate who had written a magnum opus. Or, if you were some celebrated politician with a revealing memoir. Or, if as a scientist, you had written a book about how time travels backward, entitled *The Theory of Backward Movement*. All of the above publishers I have mentioned, and others not named, would rush to dangle certified bank checks with ten digit figures before your smiling face! But try sending your unsolicited manuscript, you unknown writer, and be damned!

Let's illustrate this point further. Do you know Jerzy Kosinski's *The Thirty-Nine Steps*? Yes, one writer had that bestseller typed, and submitted, as a manuscript by a new writer, and waited for an answer. And what reply did he get? All the trade publishers and agents rejected it. And to worsen the experiment, Random House, which originally published the book, threw it out as an insignificant manuscript. Yet, this was a National Book Award Winner!

Some other bestsellers were "randomly" rejected like *The Jungle* by Upton Sinclair, Thomas Paine's *Common Sense*, and *The Magnificent Obsession* by Lloyd C. Douglas.

Subsidy Publishers

Also known as private, commission, or vanity publishers, subsidy publishers are a better choice if you can pay to get your book published. And they pay higher commission or royalties than the trade publishers. Vantage Press (U.S.) and Minerva Press (UK) are subsidy publishers.

Here you have control over content and price, and you get up to 40 percent royalty after sales. But you have to pay to have your work published.

Paying for book publication has a long history. Many great writers started that way. Edward Fitzgerald financed the publication of his monumental work, *The Rubaiyat of Omar Khayyam*. Thomas Gray paid to publish his classic, *Elegy*. Edgar Allan Poe sponsored the printing of the book of all times, *Tamerlane and other Poems*. And Leo Tolstoy paid for the publication of the best novel on earth, *War and Peace.*

The list also includes Thomas Hardy, Alexander Pope, T.S. Eliot, Alfred Lord Tennyson and many others. They all paid to publish their works.

Self Publishing

You may decide to do it yourself. Print and publish your work. Go round, promote and distribute your book. Become your own manager, accountant, and clerk.

Then ask yourself: *How far can I go? Do I have the time? Do I have the experience? Can I bear the health and physical risks?*

If none of the above appeals to you, do not tuck away your precious manuscript in the attic and go bungee jumping! So why not try the exciting world of online publishing.

CHAPTER 14

ONLINE PUBLISHING

"The more things change, the more they remain the same."—Alphonse Karr

Publishing has now gone online with the advent of the Internet. The following two options are available for the author:

E-book Publishers

They make your book available electronically for download. E-book publication has many advantages and disadvantages. It provides the finest opportunity for any writer to test the viability of their work.

You can gain attention and move on to the big publishing houses after your e-book is published.

Consider the following:

The journey of the millionaire author E.L. James began as an online publisher. The trilogy *Fifty Shades of Grey* started as an electronic book. Now it is an international bestseller.

M.J. Rose whose real name is Melisse Shapiro first published *Lip Service* on the Web as an e-book in 1998 after several rejections by publishers. The book sold moderately and she went on to print 3,000 paperback copies. She later got a contract with Pocket Books—making her the first online author to clinch a book deal. Now, *Lip Service* has sold over 40,000 copies and Pocket Books has signed a contract with her for *In Fidelity* her next novel

After Arthur C. Clarke published a six-page story which sold online through fatbrain.com, Stephen King went on to experiment the form with *Riding the Bullet*, a 66-page short story that got over 500,000 readers downloading and making the author $450,000 richer. Now he is selling a full-length novel online in installments.

The bad side of e-books is that it presents marketing problem. Again, editors do not like reviewing them—they prefer a physical copy. And writers do not bother to edit their e-books, making it hard for readers to take such works seriously.

However, electronic books are now selling faster than paperbacks.

You can register and publish your e-books free in the following sites:

https://kdp.amazon.com

http://www.pubit.barnesandnoble.com

http://www.smashwords.com

Most sites automatically convert your MS Word manuscript to e-book while some require a pdf copy.

If you want your e-book to make you money, professionally format, design, edit, and promote it before and after publication.

Print-on-Demand Publishers

These are the subsidy publishers on the Internet but it has some advantages.

The book is only printed and shipped to you when you order. There are no unsold copies. It also costs less to publish a POD book and it takes a very short time to produce.

There are disadvantages of this type of publishing. Your book may be distributed to online bookstores worldwide. But there is no concerted effort to generate orders for the book. It is also pertinent to know that physical bookstores and libraries do not accept POD books.

This is partly because the book quality and cover image of most POD books is poor. Also, it is not the business of the publisher to publicize and market your book. This is in addition to the fact that the cost of one POD book can quadruple a lithographic copy.

POD publishing can be viewed as a stepping-stone to recognition if you can promote and market your book. After all, Stephen King didn't just happen. He is still publishing and selling online.

Do you need a POD publisher? Go to:

http://hipiers.com/publishing.html

http://www.createspace.com

There is something however that is more important than writing and publishing a book. What is it?

CHAPTER 15

HOW TO PROMOTE YOUR BOOK

"Thunder is good, thunder is fine, but it is lightning that does all the work."—Mark Twain

It is good to know all the rules of writing bestsellers and to be acquainted with the style of bestselling authors. It is also a wonderful thing to be published. But it is promotion—getting the 7 billion people out there to know that you have arrived—that is the titanic task!

We will now discuss ways to promote and market your book for best results.

Get your book listed

This is perhaps the first thing to be done as soon as your book is released so that your readers can readily find it. You can have it listed for distribution below:

http://www.bookmarket.com/distributors.html

Word of Mouth

It may surprise you, but word of mouth is the cheapest and best type of advertising. The point is that 95 percent of people like to share the new things that they have learnt with relatives and friends.

Your first task therefore will be to make your published work available to as many people as possible. Then gossip takes over.

There are several instances where word of mouth worked magic.

Let's consider one. When Edward Fitzgerald wrote *The Rubaiyat of Omar Khayyam* he may never have known that he would sell. The author kept 100 copies in the window of a local bookstore. Then what happened?

It caught the attention of the poet and painter, Dante Gabriel Rossetti, who after reading it, bought all copies of the book, and gave them to his friends. And so started the incredible success story of *The Rubaiyat.*

Traditional advertising

Publishers use advertising methods that are most effective for their situations. Some common promotion methods are through catalogs, sales to bookstores, libraries, schools, organizations, and other institutions.

Wholesalers and book distributors

You will need wholesalers and book distributors to circulate your published book. Remember that distributors and editors don't touch POD books.,

Book reviews and press releases

Use book reviews, press releases, free and paid ads in print and electronic media and window displays to announce the arrival of your book.

Book fair and trade shows

In addition, book fairs, trade shows, and gift shows could form an excellent opportunity to put your book in the hand of readers. Attend, showcase, and give away your book.

Online advertising

You must have an online presence as a writer. A reader must be able to find information about you and your work by searching the Web. This can be done by creating a professional website or blog for your work.

Also, circulate information about your book online. These can be in form of free chapters, articles, essays, press releases, reviews, e-mail marketing, discussion groups/forums, or through chat rooms—giving you the initial publicity that you need in your book promo effort. Remember to include your byline/signature and your book's landing page/link in your posts. That is guaranteed visits and sales for life.

Autograph Parties

You, your publisher, or bookstore, may arrange autograph parties or book signings.

Publicize the event and have sufficient quantities of books to go round. Apart from autographing books, make a show out of it—pose for photographs with your guests and see that the reporters are there to publish the story!

Public Presentation

The public presentation or launching of your book can be a great opportunity to advertise it. Make a pre-event publicity and then on the event date, do a press conference. Also entertain your invited guests. You might make money from those that might buy your book on that day. But even if you don't, the publicity will eventually help to market the book.

Grant Interviews

Reporters are always looking for celebrities to interview. Yes, be press friendly; grant interviews. But note that you have to know what to say before granting interviews. Also, note that the interview is a means of letting the public to know more about you and your works. So give answers that will help your readers understand you better.

Know your purpose of being there—promotion. You will therefore not fail to drop the title of your book several times. You can also make the interview memorable by giving illustrations, or telling stories, and even provoking a debate that will continue after the interview.

Author Tours / Talks

Take a tour of public institutions, prepare, and give good talks to large audiences. You should have mastery of your topic, and in giving the talk, you should know that your personal appearance, gestures, and audience contact, are very important. You may also take questions at the end of the talk. But the most important thing is that you will get paid for promoting your book!

Offer Serialization / Reprint

When your book is published, make limited chapters available free to create awareness. It can be online or in a physical newspaper or magazine. If you have a good story, you would have created a demand for your book.

Charles Dickens started that way. He serialized his early work in The Pickwick Papers for general reading before he gained renown.

Hire a Publicist

It is true that even with your best effort there are some things you may not know about book marketing. You therefore have to hire a book marketer or a book publicity agent to do a professional job for you. Even though it might be costly for you to do so, it is worthwhile.

A publicist will take your work to top TV talk shows, cable TV networks, big newspapers and news syndicates.

Social Networking Sites

Share and post information about your book on the following sites:

http://www.facebook.com

http://www.twitter.com

http://www.stumbleupon.com

http://www.linkedin.com

http://www.digg.com

http://www.reddit.com

Literary Sites

Post your book information on the sites below:

http://www.librarything.com

http://www.goodreads.com

http://www.shelfari.com

http://www.bookcrossings.com

Find literary opportunities for your book below:

http://www.literarymarkeplace.com

Marketing websites

Use marketing sites to know how and where to market your work. Try these:

http://www.marketability.com

http://www.bookmarket.com

Mailing list

E-mail marketing is good. But good lists are hard to come by and are not cheap. I will recommend the site below:

http://www.bookmarket.com/lists.htm

Newsletters

Subscribe to and read writing and publishing newsletters to keep you informed about the latest in the trade. Read Publishers Weekly, Write101.com, John Kremer, and BookPros.

Facebook Ad

Advertise your book to the over 1 billion monthly users by clicking below:

http://www.facebook.com/ads/create/

Yahoo Ad

Advertise on yahoo below:

http://www.advertising.yahoo.com

Google AdWords

Use Google AdWords and reach your target readers. To learn more, click below:

http://www.adwords.google.com

Google Alerts

Use Google alerts to trace your marketing campaign. This will inform you of every mention of your name, book title, review, article, or interview. Create one below:

http://www.google.com/alerts

You might feel that all of these efforts are daunting. But you can't be a celeb without hard work just as you can't make an omelet without breaking eggs.

Why don't you then make the effort needed to promote your work? Perhaps you may succeed.